The Art of Letting Go

Your Comprehensive Manual to Downsizing and Living Light

Taylor Woods

Table of contents

Chapter1: The Clutter Conundrum

In the chaos of modern living, the Clutter Conundrum emerges as a pervasive challenge, impacting our mental well-being and the sanctity of our spaces. It's more than a mere physical presence; clutter infiltrates our minds, subtly influencing our thoughts, emotions, and actions.

Unveiling the Clutter Phenomenon

At its core, clutter isn't merely an accumulation of possessions; it's a reflection of our inner state. It's the physical manifestation of indecision, procrastination, and an attachment to the past or an uncertain future. The Clutter Conundrum, therefore, isn't solely about tidying up; it's about understanding the psychology behind our attachment to things.

The Psychological Impact of Clutter

Research delves deep into the psychological effects of clutter on our mental health. It's more than a messy room; it's a constant source of stress, anxiety, and even feelings of guilt. The weight of clutter hampers creativity, productivity, and overall well-being. As clutter accumulates, it silently but significantly impacts our ability to focus, make decisions, and find peace within our spaces.

Identifying the Root Causes

To unravel the Clutter Conundrum, we must delve into its origins. It often stems from a fear of letting go, an emotional attachment to possessions, societal pressures, or a quest for identity through material belongings. Understanding these underlying causes empowers us to address clutter at its source.

A Mindful Approach to Decluttering

The solution lies not merely in tidying but in a shift
of mindset. Mindful decluttering involves a
deliberate, conscious effort to evaluate possessions
based on your true value in our lives. It requires us
to question our attachments, assess functionality,
and discern between necessity and excess.

Strategies for Liberation

This chapter offers an array of actionable strategies.
From the KonMari method's joy-sparking approach
to the minimalist principle of intentional living,
each strategy equips individuals with tools to
confront the clutter and restore harmony.

Cultivating a Clutter-Free Mindset

Breaking free from the Clutter Conundrum
involves adopting a mindset of simplicity, focusing

on experiences over possessions, and cherishing the present moment. This shift unlocks the doors to a lighter, more fulfilling existence, unencumbered by the weight of unnecessary belongings.

Finding Peace in Spaces

As we embark on this journey of decluttering, we rediscover the joy of space. Each cleared surface becomes a canvas for inspiration, every organized corner a sanctuary for peace. Creating harmonious spaces allows room for growth, creativity, and a renewed sense of tranquility.

Conclusion

The Clutter Conundrum isn't an insurmountable challenge; it's an invitation to introspect and transform. By understanding its psychological underpinnings, embracing mindful practices, and nurturing a clutter-free mindset, we pave the way for a life of simplicity, purpose, and profound contentment.

Chapter2: Embracing the Minimalist Mindset

In a world often defined by excess and accumulation, the Minimalist Mindset stands as a beacon of simplicity, inviting individuals to reassess your relationship with possessions, values, and the very essence of a meaningful life. This chapter embarks on a profound exploration of the transformative power inherent in adopting and fully embracing the Minimalist Mindset.

The Essence of Minimalism

At its core, minimalism is more than an aesthetic choice; it's a deliberate and intentional way of life. It challenges the societal norms that equate success with material wealth and advocates for a recalibration of priorities, urging individuals to focus on what truly matters.

Beyond Materialism: Redefining Success

The journey to embracing a minimalist mindset begins with a reevaluation of the traditional markers of success. Instead of measuring worth through possessions, individuals are encouraged to consider the value of experiences, relationships, and personal growth. This paradigm shift forms the foundation of the minimalist ethos.

Mindful Consumption: Quality Over Quantity

A central tenet of the Minimalist Mindset is the practice of mindful consumption. This involves a deliberate and conscious approach to acquiring possessions, emphasizing quality over quantity. By selecting items that truly add value and joy to one's life, the clutter of excess is replaced with purposeful, curated belongings.

The Freedom of Letting Go

Minimalism encourages individuals to shed the weight of unnecessary possessions, fostering a sense of liberation. Letting go of the superfluous allows for a clearer focus on what truly matters, creating space for personal growth, creativity, and a deeper connection to the present moment.

Building a Minimalist Home: The Art of Simplicity

This chapter delves into the practical aspects of creating a minimalist home. From decluttering techniques to mindful organization strategies, you are guided through the process of transforming your living spaces into sanctuaries of simplicity. The minimalist home becomes a reflection of the intentional choices made in pursuit of a more meaningful life.

The Minimalist Wardrobe: Dressing with Purpose

A minimalist mindset extends to the wardrobe, promoting the creation of a capsule collection that is both functional and reflective of personal style. The chapter explores the benefits of a streamlined wardrobe, including reduced decision fatigue, increased self-awareness, and a sustainable approach to fashion.

Digital Detox: Simplifying the Virtual Space

In the digital age, a minimalist mindset extends beyond physical possessions to the virtual realm. Strategies for a digital detox are presented, empowering individuals to declutter your digital lives, establish healthy boundaries with technology, and cultivate a more mindful and intentional online presence.

Minimalism as a Lifestyle: Sustainable Practices

As you fully embrace the Minimalist Mindset, this chapter introduces sustainable practices that align with a minimalist lifestyle. From eco-friendly consumption habits to waste reduction strategies, the journey toward minimalism becomes synonymous with responsible and conscientious living.

Cultivating Mindfulness: A Daily Practice

The chapter concludes by emphasizing that embracing the Minimalist Mindset is an ongoing, mindful practice. By integrating the principles of minimalism into daily life, individuals can experience lasting benefits, including increased clarity, reduced stress, and a profound sense of contentment.

In the symphony of modern living, the Minimalist Mindset emerges as a harmonious melody, inviting individuals to simplify, prioritize, and rediscover the true essence of a purposeful and fulfilling life.

Chapter3: Starting Small: The 30-Day Challenge

The journey to decluttering and embracing a minimalist lifestyle often feels daunting, overwhelming, and even unattainable. The idea of tackling years of accumulated belongings in one go can be paralyzing. Recognizing this, the 30-Day Challenge emerges as a transformative tool, a gradual and manageable approach to initiating significant change in one's life.

The Concept of the 30-Day Challenge

At its essence, the 30-Day Challenge embodies the philosophy of starting small to achieve big results. It harnesses the power of incremental progress, breaking down a seemingly monumental task into bite-sized, actionable steps that can be easily integrated into daily life.

Setting the Stage: Preparing for Success

Before embarking on the challenge, it's crucial to set the stage for success. This involves creating a personalized plan, defining specific goals, and visualizing the desired outcomes. Additionally, establishing a supportive environment and mindset lays the groundwork for a successful 30-day journey.

Day-by-Day Breakdown: A Comprehensive Guide

The 30-Day Challenge unfolds as a structured roadmap, guiding participants through a series of daily tasks, each designed to chip away at the clutter and foster a minimalist mindset.

Days 1-5: Identifying Priorities
These initial days focus on self-reflection and goal setting. Participants evaluate your values, priorities,

and aspirations, laying the groundwork for informed decision-making throughout the challenge.

Days 6-10: Room-by-Room Evaluation
  Participants systematically assess your living spaces, beginning with one room at a time. They identify areas for decluttering, categorize possessions, and initiate the process of letting go.

Days 11-15: Mindful Decluttering
  Armed with newfound clarity, individuals delve deeper into decluttering. They embrace a mindful approach, evaluating possessions based on utility, sentimental value, or your alignment with personal goals.

Days 16-20: Organizing and Optimizing
  With a reduced inventory, focus shifts to organizing the remaining belongings. Participants explore effective organizational strategies to

optimize your spaces, enhancing functionality and aesthetics.

Days 21-25: Reflecting and Adjusting
 The midpoint prompts a pause for reflection. Participants assess your progress, identify challenges, and make any necessary adjustments to your approach.

Days 26-30: Consolidation and Celebration
 The final stretch involves consolidating efforts, completing any remaining tasks, and celebrating achievements. Participants reflect on the transformation and establish plans to maintain your newfound minimalist lifestyle.

Benefits Beyond Decluttering

Beyond the physical act of decluttering, the 30-Day Challenge offers an array of benefits. Participants experience increased clarity of mind, reduced stress, enhanced decision-making skills, and a newfound appreciation for simplicity.

Sustainable Change and Long-Term Impact

The 30-Day Challenge serves as a catalyst for sustainable change. By ingraining new habits, fostering a minimalist mindset, and experiencing the tangible benefits of a clutter-free environment, participants lay the foundation for lasting transformation.

Conclusion: A Stepping Stone to a Minimalist Lifestyle

As the 30 days draw to a close, participants are not merely concluding a challenge; they are inaugurating a new chapter in your lives. The lessons learned, habits formed, and perspectives shifted during this journey serve as stepping stones toward a more intentional, purposeful, and fulfilling minimalist lifestyle.

Chapter4: The Power of Positivity in Decluttering

In the pursuit of a clutter-free and harmonious existence, the role of positivity emerges as a guiding force, wielding transformative influence throughout the decluttering process. This chapter embarks on an exploration of how cultivating a positive mindset can profoundly impact the decluttering journey, fostering a sense of empowerment, clarity, and renewed purpose.

Understanding the Role of Positivity

Positivity serves as more than a mere emotional state; it becomes a catalyst for change. When applied to the decluttering process, it infuses every decision and action with optimism, resilience, and an unwavering belief in the possibilities of a simplified life.

The Mind-Clutter Connection

Acknowledging the intricate link between the mind and external environment is crucial. A cluttered space often mirrors a cluttered mind, and vice versa. Positivity, therefore, serves as a key to unlock the symbiotic relationship between decluttering physical spaces and achieving mental clarity.

The Art of Mindful Decision-Making

Positivity guides individuals through the intricate process of decision-making during decluttering. It instills confidence in assessing belongings, discerning your value, and making choices that align with personal goals. By adopting a positive perspective, individuals can navigate the emotional attachments to possessions with grace and ease.

Harnessing the Power of Gratitude

Gratitude emerges as a potent tool in the decluttering arsenal. By cultivating a mindset of gratitude for the items that have served your purpose, individuals can bid farewell to possessions with a sense of appreciation rather than regret. This shift in perspective fosters a lighter emotional load throughout the decluttering journey.

Positivity as a Motivational Driver

Amidst the challenges inherent in decluttering, positivity acts as a source of motivation and resilience. It fuels momentum, inspiring individuals to persevere through moments of doubt or fatigue. A positive outlook nurtures the belief that every discarded item paves the way for a more fulfilling and purpose-driven life.

Creating Positive Spaces: The Ripple Effect

As decluttering progresses, spaces transform into havens of positivity. Clearing physical clutter creates room for positive energy to flow freely, fostering an environment conducive to peace, creativity, and overall well-being. Each organized space becomes a canvas for a more harmonious existence.

Cultivating a Positive Lifestyle Beyond Decluttering

The journey of decluttering transcends physical spaces; it extends to lifestyle choices. Embracing positivity as a way of life fosters a holistic approach to wellness, encouraging individuals to surround themselves with positivity in relationships, habits, and experiences.

Sustaining Positivity in a Minimalist Lifestyle

Positivity becomes an integral part of sustaining a minimalist lifestyle. By nurturing an optimistic outlook, individuals continuously reinforce your commitment to simplicity, ensuring that positivity remains the cornerstone of your ongoing journey toward a clutter-free and purposeful existence.

Conclusion: Embracing Positivity for Lasting Transformation

In conclusion, the power of positivity permeates every facet of the decluttering process. By embracing positivity, individuals not only declutter your physical spaces but also declutter your minds, paving the way for a life imbued with clarity, intentionality, and boundless positivity.

Chapter5: Sorting Through Sentiment: Navigating Emotional Attachments

In the journey toward a minimalist lifestyle, one of the most intricate and emotionally charged aspects is the process of sorting through sentimental belongings. This chapter delves into the profound and often challenging task of navigating emotional attachments, offering you a thoughtful guide on how to strike a balance between cherishing memories and embracing the liberating power of letting go.

The Complexity of Sentimental Attachments

Sentimental belongings carry a weight beyond your physical presence. They are imbued with memories, emotions, and stories that make parting with them a complex and emotionally charged endeavor. Understanding this complexity is the first step toward navigating the intricate landscape of sentimental decluttering.

Unpacking the Emotional Baggage

As you embark on the journey of sorting through sentimental items, the chapter encourages them to unpack the emotional baggage associated with each possession. By recognizing the emotions tied to specific items, individuals can address them consciously, separating the essence of the memory from the physical object.

The Power of Mindful Reflection

Mindful reflection becomes a crucial tool in navigating emotional attachments. This chapter provides exercises and prompts to guide you in exploring the significance of sentimental items. Through thoughtful contemplation, individuals gain insights into which memories truly enrich your lives and which may be ready to be honored and released.

Preserving Memories without Physical Clutter

A central theme emerges: it's possible to preserve cherished memories without being tethered to physical clutter. The chapter explores creative ways to document and celebrate memories, from digital photo albums to curated memory boxes. These alternatives offer a middle ground where sentimentality is honored without compromising the pursuit of a minimalist lifestyle.

Establishing Criteria for Keep or Release

The chapter introduces practical criteria to aid you in discerning whether to keep or release sentimental items. By evaluating the significance of an item in relation to personal values and future aspirations, individuals can make informed decisions that align with your overall goals of simplification and mindful living.

The Ritual of Letting Go

Acknowledging that letting go is a process, not an event, the chapter explores rituals that can make the process more intentional and meaningful. Whether through gratitude ceremonies or acts of generosity, these rituals transform the act of decluttering into a transformative and empowering experience.

Compassion for the Past Self

An empathetic perspective toward one's past self is crucial in navigating sentimental attachments. The chapter encourages you to approach your younger selves with compassion, recognizing that the person who held onto certain items may have been motivated by different needs, desires, or circumstances.

Seeking Support and Guidance

Navigating emotional attachments can be a solitary journey, but it doesn't have to be. The chapter discusses the importance of seeking support and guidance from friends, family, or even professional organizers. Shared experiences and insights can provide emotional support and practical advice during this introspective process.

Celebrating the Liberation

The chapter concludes with a celebration of the liberation that comes with successfully navigating emotional attachments. By letting go of what no longer serves a purpose, individuals make space for new experiences, personal growth, and a lighter, more joyful existence. The act of decluttering sentimental items becomes a profound gesture of self-love and intentional living.

In the delicate dance of sorting through sentiment, this chapter serves as a compassionate guide, empowering you to navigate the emotional complexities with wisdom and grace. Through mindful reflection and intentional choices, individuals can emerge not only with decluttered spaces but also with a deeper understanding of themselves and a renewed appreciation for the beauty of letting go.

Chapter6: Practical Purging: Streamlining Your Possessions

The process of purging possessions represents a fundamental step toward achieving a clutter-free and purposeful lifestyle. This chapter embarks on an in-depth exploration of practical purging, offering you comprehensive strategies, techniques, and insights to effectively streamline your possessions and pave the way for a more intentional and simplified life.

Understanding the Philosophy of Purging

At its core, purging possessions involves a deliberate and systematic approach to decluttering. It's not merely about discarding items but about conscientiously evaluating belongings, determining your value, and curating a collection that aligns with one's goals and values. This chapter delves into the philosophical underpinnings of purging and its transformative potential.

The Art of Categorization and Assessment

Central to the process of practical purging is the art of categorization and assessment. you are guided through methods for categorizing possessions based on utility, sentimental value, frequency of use, and alignment with personal aspirations. By systematically evaluating each category, individuals gain clarity on which items contribute meaningfully to your lives.

The Joy-Sparking Principle: Marie Kondo's Method

The chapter introduces the renowned joy-sparking principle popularized by Marie Kondo. This method prompts individuals to assess possessions based on the emotions they evoke, encouraging them to keep items that bring joy and release those that no longer resonate positively. Practical tips and exercises based on this principle empower you to apply this approach effectively.

Tactical Techniques for Decluttering

This section of the chapter dives deep into practical techniques for decluttering. From the tried-and-tested "one in, one out" rule to the "box method" for undecided items, you discover actionable strategies to streamline possessions methodically, ensuring a manageable and sustainable purging process.

The Role of Mindfulness in Purging

Mindfulness emerges as a guiding principle throughout the purging journey. By cultivating a mindful approach, individuals navigate the emotional complexities of letting go, make informed decisions, and appreciate the present moment. Techniques for practicing mindfulness during purging are explored to foster a sense of presence and intentionality.

Overcoming Purging Roadblocks

Purging possessions may encounter roadblocks, such as sentimental attachments, guilt, or fear of scarcity. This chapter equips you with tools to overcome these obstacles. From reframing perspectives on sentimental items to addressing underlying beliefs about possessions, individuals are empowered to navigate these challenges effectively.

Organizing and Managing Purged Items

Successfully purging possessions is only part of the process; effectively managing the purged items is equally crucial. This section discusses strategies for responsible disposal, donation, or repurposing of items, ensuring that the decluttered space remains clutter-free and sustainable.

Creating Systems for Maintenance

To sustain the benefits of purging, the chapter concludes with insights into establishing systems for ongoing maintenance. From setting boundaries on acquiring new possessions to regular reassessment of belongings, you learn how to integrate purging as an ongoing practice in your lives.

Conclusion: The Transformative Power of Practical Purging

In summary, practical purging is not merely about decluttering possessions; it's a transformative journey toward intentional living. By embracing systematic evaluation, mindful decision-making, and responsible management of belongings, individuals pave the way for a life enriched by purpose, clarity, and the freedom that comes from owning only what truly matters.

Chapter7: Space Liberation: Optimizing Your Living Environment

Cultivating Clarity Through Organization

Optimizing your living environment begins with organization as its cornerstone. This section explores the transformative power of intentional organization. you discover practical strategies for decluttering and organizing your spaces to enhance functionality, efficiency, and aesthetic appeal. From implementing storage solutions that maximize space utilization to establishing daily habits that maintain order, this chapter offers actionable techniques to cultivate a sense of clarity and purpose within your surroundings. Emphasizing the link between an organized space and mental clarity, you learn how a well-organized environment fosters a sense of calm and facilitates better focus, productivity, and overall well-being.

Harmonizing Design and Functionality

This section delves into the art of harmonizing design with functionality. It guides you through the process of creating spaces that not only look aesthetically pleasing but also serve your intended purposes efficiently. By exploring principles of interior design, ergonomic layouts, and personalized styling, individuals learn how to craft living environments that reflect your unique personalities while optimizing usability. The chapter underscores the importance of balance, encouraging you to strike a harmonious blend between beauty and functionality in your living spaces. Through insightful perspectives and practical strategies, you gain the tools to transform your environments into inviting, purposeful, and well-designed sanctuaries.

Cultivating Mindfulness in Your Space

This segment highlights the profound connection between mindfulness and living environments. you are introduced to the concept of mindfulness in spatial design, emphasizing the importance of being present and intentional in every aspect of space utilization. From incorporating elements that promote relaxation and mindfulness to creating designated areas for reflection and rejuvenation, individuals discover how intentional design choices can contribute to a sense of tranquility and balance. This section also explores the concept of minimalist living, encouraging you to curate spaces intentionally by focusing on essentials and eliminating distractions. By cultivating mindfulness in your living environments, you learn to foster a deeper appreciation for the spaces they inhabit and create surroundings that support your emotional, mental, and spiritual well-being.

In the pursuit of space liberation, this chapter acts as a guide, empowering you to transform your living environments into harmonious, organized, and mindful spaces that elevate your quality of life. Through practical strategies, insightful perspectives, and a deep understanding of the profound connection between space and well-being, individuals are equipped to embark on a journey of optimizing their living environments for greater clarity, functionality, and peace.

Chapter8: The Art of Digital Detox: Streamlining Your Virtual World

Cultivating Awareness in Digital Consumption

The chapter begins by exploring the significance of cultivating awareness in digital consumption. It delves into the pervasive nature of technology in modern life and its impact on mental well-being. you gain insights into recognizing excessive digital consumption patterns and understanding the potential consequences, such as increased stress, reduced productivity, and decreased focus. Practical strategies are introduced to cultivate mindfulness in digital usage, including setting boundaries, practicing tech-free times, and mindful engagement with technology. By fostering awareness, individuals can regain control over their digital habits, creating a healthier relationship with technology that promotes balance and intentionality.

Streamlining Digital Spaces for Productivity and Clarity

This section delves into the art of streamlining digital spaces for enhanced productivity and mental clarity. you discover practical strategies to declutter digital environments, such as organizing files, managing emails, and minimizing distractions. Insights into effective digital organization tools and techniques are provided, empowering individuals to optimize your virtual spaces for improved efficiency and focus. The chapter emphasizes the importance of digital minimalism, encouraging you to curate your digital lives intentionally by reducing unnecessary apps, subscriptions, and notifications. By streamlining your virtual world, individuals create an environment conducive to productivity, creativity, and mental clarity.

Nurturing a Balanced Digital Lifestyle

The final segment explores the concept of nurturing a balanced digital lifestyle. It introduces the idea of striking a healthy equilibrium between technology use and offline experiences. you learn practical strategies to establish boundaries, such as setting designated tech-free zones or engaging in digital sabbaticals. The chapter encourages individuals to explore alternative activities that promote well-being, such as hobbies, mindfulness practices, or spending quality time with loved ones. By nurturing a balanced digital lifestyle, individuals can reclaim their time, reduce stress, and foster deeper connections with themselves and others, ultimately leading to a more fulfilling and balanced existence.

In the pursuit of a digital detox, this chapter serves as a comprehensive guide, offering practical strategies, insightful perspectives, and a deep understanding of the profound connection between digital habits and well-being. Through cultivating awareness, streamlining digital spaces, and nurturing a balanced digital lifestyle, you are empowered to regain control over your virtual world, fostering a healthier and more intentional relationship with technology.

Chapter9: Eco-Friendly Downsizing: Reducing Your Environmental Footprint

Understanding the Environmental Impact of Consumerism

The chapter commences by exploring the significant environmental implications of consumerism and excessive consumption. It delves into the environmental footprint associated with a culture of mass consumption, highlighting issues such as resource depletion, pollution, waste generation, and climate change. you gain insights into the interconnectedness between consumption habits, environmental degradation, and the urgent need for sustainable practices.

Understanding the magnitude of individual contributions to environmental issues sets the stage for individuals to embark on the journey of eco-friendly downsizing. It lays the groundwork for you to reassess your consumption patterns and make informed choices that positively impact the environment.

Strategies for Sustainable Downsizing

This section introduces practical strategies for eco-friendly downsizing, focusing on reducing one's environmental impact while transitioning to a simpler lifestyle. you are presented with actionable steps, such as minimizing waste through recycling, composting, and reducing single-use plastics. Insights into energy conservation, water efficiency, and conscious transportation choices are provided, empowering individuals to make eco-conscious decisions in various aspects of their lives.

The chapter also explores the principles of minimalism and mindful consumption as integral components of eco-friendly downsizing. It encourages you to prioritize quality over quantity, embrace second-hand and sustainable products, and practice conscious consumerism. By incorporating these strategies into your daily lives, individuals can significantly reduce your environmental footprint while embracing a simpler and more sustainable lifestyle.

Cultivating a Culture of Sustainability

The final segment delves into the broader implications of eco-friendly downsizing in cultivating a culture of sustainability. It emphasizes the importance of collective action and community engagement in creating meaningful change. you are encouraged to advocate for sustainable practices in your communities, support environmentally responsible businesses, and participate in initiatives promoting environmental conservation and eco-friendly lifestyles.

This section also explores the role of education and awareness in fostering a culture of sustainability. It highlights the significance of educating oneself and others about the environmental impact of consumption habits, inspiring individuals to become advocates for positive environmental change within your spheres of influence.

By cultivating a culture of sustainability, individuals not only reduce their own environmental footprint but also contribute to a larger movement toward a more ecologically balanced and sustainable world.

In the pursuit of eco-friendly downsizing, this chapter serves as a comprehensive guide, offering practical strategies, insightful perspectives, and a deep understanding of the profound connection between consumption habits and environmental impact. Through understanding environmental implications, adopting sustainable downsizing strategies, and cultivating a culture of sustainability, you are empowered to reduce your environmental footprint and contribute to a more sustainable future.

Chapter 10: Creating Harmony in the Home: Feng Shui for Minimalists

Understanding Feng Shui as a Path to Harmony

The chapter begins by exploring the ancient Chinese philosophy of Feng Shui and its profound connection to creating harmony in the home. you are introduced to the core principles of Feng Shui, which revolves around the idea that the arrangement and organization of our living spaces profoundly impact our energy, well-being, and overall quality of life. The concept of Qi, the life force energy, is central to Feng Shui, emphasizing the importance of balancing and harmonizing the energies within our homes.

Understanding Feng Shui as a tool for creating harmony lays the foundation for individuals, especially minimalists, to appreciate how intentional design and organization can positively influence your living environments. The principles of Feng Shui align seamlessly with minimalist values, promoting simplicity, balance, and a mindful approach to space.

Minimalist Feng Shui: Balancing Elements and Energies

This section delves into the application of Feng Shui principles within a minimalist framework. you discover practical strategies for incorporating Feng Shui into your minimalist lifestyle, emphasizing the balance of the five essential elements: wood, fire, earth, metal, and water. Practical tips for creating a harmonious balance include incorporating natural materials, embracing a clutter-free environment, and organizing spaces mindfully.

Insights into the Bagua map, an essential tool in Feng Shui, are provided, guiding you in mapping out the energy centers within your homes. By aligning minimalist principles with the Bagua map, individuals can ensure that each area of your living space reflects your intentions and supports your overall well-being.

 The Mindful Minimalist Home: A Haven of Harmony

The final segment explores the concept of the mindful minimalist home as a haven of harmony. It delves into the importance of cultivating mindfulness in every aspect of the living environment, from the arrangement of furniture to the choice of colors and decor. you are encouraged to approach the creation of your minimalist haven with intentionality, considering not only the visual aesthetics but also the energy flow and the emotions evoked by your surroundings.

Practical strategies for achieving harmony in a minimalist home are presented, including the strategic placement of furniture, the use of mirrors to enhance energy flow, and the incorporation of plants for a touch of nature. The chapter also emphasizes the significance of decluttering and organizing mindfully, ensuring that each item serves a purpose and contributes positively to the overall ambiance.

By aligning the principles of minimalist living with the wisdom of Feng Shui, individuals can transform their homes into sanctuaries of harmony, where energy flows seamlessly, and every element contributes to a sense of balance, peace, and well-being.

In the pursuit of creating harmony in the home through Feng Shui for minimalists, this chapter serves as a comprehensive guide, offering practical strategies, insightful perspectives, and a deep understanding of the profound connection between intentional design and overall well-being. Through understanding Feng Shui principles, implementing minimalist Feng Shui practices, and cultivating a mindful minimalist home, you are empowered to create living environments that not only reflect your minimalist values but also radiate harmony and balance.

Chapter11: Capsule Wardrobe Magic: Dressing with Intention

Unveiling the Essence of a Capsule Wardrobe

The chapter opens by unraveling the essence of a capsule wardrobe, a concept centered on dressing with intentionality and minimalism. It introduces you to the philosophy behind the capsule wardrobe, emphasizing the principles of quality over quantity, versatility, and curated simplicity. By distilling one's wardrobe to a collection of essential, timeless, and interchangeable pieces, individuals unlock a world of possibilities and effortlessly curated style.

Understanding the transformative power of a capsule wardrobe sets the stage for individuals to embrace intentional dressing, transcending the cycle of excessive consumption and trend-driven fashion. It lays the foundation for a more conscious and mindful approach to personal style, where each garment serves a purpose and contributes to a cohesive, versatile, and effortlessly chic wardrobe.

Crafting Your Signature Style: The Capsule Wardrobe Approach

This section delves into the practical strategies and insights for crafting a signature style through the capsule wardrobe approach. you discover actionable steps for curating your capsule wardrobe, starting with decluttering and assessing your existing clothing items. Insights into selecting timeless and versatile pieces, creating color palettes, and focusing on quality, fit, and functionality are provided, empowering individuals to build a wardrobe that aligns with your lifestyle and personal aesthetic.

The chapter also explores the art of mixing and matching within a capsule wardrobe, showcasing the versatility and endless outfit combinations that can be achieved with a curated collection of garments. It encourages you to embrace creativity and experiment with layering, accessories, and varied styling techniques to express your individuality while maintaining the essence of a minimalist wardrobe.

Embracing the Mindful Wardrobe Ritual

The final segment delves into the concept of embracing a mindful wardrobe ritual as part of the capsule wardrobe journey. It emphasizes the importance of conscious purchasing habits, encouraging individuals to adopt a discerning approach when adding new pieces to your wardrobe. Strategies for mindful shopping, such as considering ethical and sustainable fashion practices, investing in timeless pieces, and practicing the "one in, one out" rule, are presented.

The chapter also addresses the emotional aspect of dressing with intention, highlighting the role of mindfulness in making deliberate wardrobe choices that evoke joy, confidence, and a sense of alignment. It encourages individuals to cultivate gratitude for your wardrobe, appreciating the value and purpose of each garment, and fostering a deeper connection with your clothing.

By embracing a mindful wardrobe ritual, individuals not only curate a capsule wardrobe but also cultivate a more mindful, sustainable, and satisfying relationship with your clothing, ultimately leading to a more intentional and harmonious approach to dressing.

In the pursuit of capsule wardrobe magic and dressing with intention, this chapter serves as a comprehensive guide, offering practical strategies, insightful perspectives, and a deep understanding of the profound connection between curated wardrobes and intentional living. Through understanding the essence of a capsule wardrobe, crafting a signature style, and embracing a mindful wardrobe ritual, you are empowered to transform your approach to dressing, discovering the magic of intentional and versatile fashion.

Chapter12: Mindful Budgeting: Financial Freedom Through Downsizing

Embracing the Mindset of Mindful Budgeting

The chapter initiates by exploring the foundational principles of mindful budgeting, emphasizing the transformative power of intentional financial practices. It delves into the essence of mindful budgeting as a mindset shift, focusing on conscious spending, prioritizing needs over wants, and aligning financial decisions with personal values and goals. You are encouraged to introspect on your relationship with money, identifying areas for improvement and recognizing the potential benefits of downsizing and simplifying your financial lives.

Understanding the mindset behind mindful budgeting sets the stage for individuals to embark on a journey towards financial freedom. It lays the groundwork for making intentional financial choices, fostering a sense of empowerment, and paving the way for a more fulfilling and purpose-driven approach to managing finances.

 Downsizing Expenses: Strategies for Financial Liberation

This section delves into practical strategies for downsizing expenses and achieving financial liberation. you are presented with actionable steps to assess your current spending habits, track expenses, and identify areas for reduction or elimination. Insights into prioritizing essential expenses, cutting unnecessary costs, and renegotiating subscriptions or services are provided, empowering individuals to optimize your budgets and allocate resources consciously.

The chapter also explores the concept of mindful consumption in the financial realm, encouraging you to question impulse purchases, embrace frugality without sacrificing quality of life, and adopt a minimalist approach to spending. By implementing these strategies, individuals can reduce financial clutter, streamline expenses, and create room for savings, ultimately fostering a sense of financial security and freedom.

Cultivating a Purposeful Financial Plan

The final segment delves into the cultivation of a purposeful financial plan rooted in mindful budgeting principles. It guides you in setting clear financial goals, whether it's building an emergency fund, paying off debts, or saving for long-term aspirations. Strategies for creating a realistic budget, setting achievable milestones, and practicing consistent review and adjustment of financial plans are discussed, enabling individuals to chart a path toward your financial objectives.

The chapter also emphasizes the importance of mindfulness in financial decision-making, encouraging you to stay present, avoid impulsive purchases, and practice gratitude for your financial resources. It underscores the idea of aligning financial choices with personal values and aspirations, fostering a sense of purpose and intentionality in financial planning.

By cultivating a purposeful financial plan through mindful budgeting, individuals not only gain control over their finances but also embark on a journey toward financial freedom and a more intentional, stress-free relationship with money.

In the pursuit of financial freedom through downsizing and mindful budgeting, this chapter serves as a comprehensive guide, offering practical strategies, insightful perspectives, and a deep understanding of the profound connection between intentional financial practices and a fulfilling life. Through embracing the mindset of mindful budgeting, downsizing expenses, and cultivating a purposeful financial plan, you are empowered to navigate your financial journeys with confidence and clarity, ultimately achieving greater financial freedom and peace of mind.

Chapter 13: Decluttering Relationships: Streamlining Social Circles

Understanding the Dynamics of Relationships

The chapter initiates by exploring the intricate dynamics of relationships, emphasizing the significance of maintaining meaningful and fulfilling connections. It delves into the complexities of social circles, highlighting the impact of relationships on mental and emotional well-being. you are encouraged to reflect on the quality of your social interactions, identifying relationships that contribute positively to your lives and those that may drain your energy or hinder personal growth.

Understanding the nuances of relationships sets the stage for individuals to embark on the process of decluttering your social circles. It lays the groundwork for evaluating the value and impact of different relationships, fostering a sense of intentionality and mindfulness in nurturing connections that truly align with one's values and aspirations.

Assessing and Prioritizing Relationships

This section delves into practical strategies for assessing and prioritizing relationships in one's social circles. You are guided through exercises to evaluate the quality and significance of your relationships, considering factors such as mutual respect, support, trust, and shared values. Insights into identifying toxic or draining relationships and setting boundaries are provided, empowering individuals to declutter relationships that no longer serve your well-being.

The chapter also encourages you to prioritize relationships that bring joy, growth, and positivity into your lives. It explores the concept of fostering deeper connections with a select few, emphasizing quality over quantity in social interactions. Strategies for nurturing meaningful relationships and investing time and energy into those that contribute positively to personal development are discussed, fostering a sense of fulfillment and support within social circles.

Cultivating a Supportive and Fulfilling Social Network

The final segment explores the cultivation of a supportive and fulfilling social network through intentional decluttering of relationships. It guides you in curating your social circles to align with your values and goals, encouraging them to seek out communities or groups that resonate with your interests, passions, or aspirations. Strategies for expanding social circles with like-minded individuals and fostering connections that foster growth and mutual support are presented.

The chapter also emphasizes the importance of effective communication and healthy conflict resolution in maintaining healthy relationships. It encourages open and honest communication, the willingness to address issues, and the ability to gracefully let go of relationships that no longer serve one's best interests.

By cultivating a supportive and fulfilling social network through decluttering relationships, individuals not only create space for meaningful connections but also foster a sense of belonging, support, and authenticity within your social circles.

In the pursuit of decluttering relationships and streamlining social circles, this chapter serves as a comprehensive guide, offering practical strategies, insightful perspectives, and a deep understanding of the profound connection between intentional relationships and personal well-being. Through understanding relationship dynamics, assessing and prioritizing connections, and cultivating a supportive social network, you are empowered to navigate your social circles with mindfulness and purpose, ultimately fostering fulfilling and enriching relationships in your lives.

Chapter14: Mindful Consumption: Breaking Free from Consumer Culture

Understanding the Grip of Consumer Culture

Consumer culture permeates our lives, shaping our identities, desires, and behaviors. This section delves into the pervasive influence of consumerism on society, highlighting its impact on individual well-being, environmental sustainability, and societal values. you gain insights into the mechanisms driving consumer culture, including advertising, social pressures, and the constant pursuit of novelty. Understanding the psychological and societal implications of consumerism lays the foundation for individuals to challenge and break free from its grip.

Consumerism often fosters a cycle of overconsumption, leading to clutter, financial strain, and environmental degradation. By recognizing the pitfalls of consumer culture, individuals can begin your journey toward mindful consumption, where intentional choices replace impulsive purchases, and value transcends material possessions.

Embracing Intentional and Ethical Choices

The chapter progresses to exploring the concept of intentional and ethical consumption as an antidote to consumer culture. you are introduced to practical strategies for cultivating mindfulness in your consumption habits. This includes conscious decision-making, such as assessing needs versus wants, researching the ethical and environmental impact of products, and prioritizing quality over quantity. Insights into minimalism, conscious consumerism, and sustainable living practices are offered, empowering individuals to make informed and responsible choices aligned with your values.

By embracing intentional and ethical consumption, individuals not only reduce your environmental footprint but also reclaim agency over your lives. This shift from mindless consumption to intentional choices fosters a sense of empowerment, satisfaction, and a deeper connection to the products and experiences that truly align with personal values and aspirations.

Cultivating a Mindful and Fulfilling Lifestyle

The final segment explores the transformative power of mindful consumption in cultivating a fulfilling lifestyle. It delves into the broader implications of mindful living, beyond consumption habits, encompassing aspects such as mindfulness practices, gratitude, and experiences over possessions. you learn to prioritize experiences that enrich your lives, foster meaningful connections, and contribute to personal growth and well-being.

This section also emphasizes the role of community and collective action in challenging consumer culture. It encourages you to participate in movements advocating for responsible consumption, supporting ethical businesses, and promoting systemic changes that prioritize sustainability and well-being over perpetual growth and consumption.

By cultivating a mindful and fulfilling lifestyle, individuals not only break free from the confines of consumer culture but also embark on a journey toward a more purposeful, connected, and contented existence.

In the pursuit of mindful consumption, this chapter serves as a comprehensive guide, offering practical strategies, insightful perspectives, and a deep understanding of the profound connection between consumption habits and personal fulfillment. Through understanding consumer culture, embracing intentional and ethical choices, and cultivating a mindful lifestyle, you are empowered to navigate a path toward mindful consumption and a more fulfilling way of living.

Chapter15: The New You: Embracing a Lighter, More Purposeful Life

The Journey Towards Transformation

The chapter opens by inviting you to embark on a transformative journey towards embracing a lighter, more purposeful life. It delves into the essence of personal transformation, emphasizing the inherent desire for growth, change, and fulfillment within individuals. you are encouraged to reflect on your current lifestyles, identifying areas for improvement and envisioning the possibilities of a more purpose-driven existence.

Understanding the essence of personal transformation sets the foundation for individuals to embark on a journey of self-discovery and growth. It lays the groundwork for embracing change, fostering a mindset of openness, and seeking new perspectives to create a life that aligns with your values and aspirations.

Shedding the Weight of Excess: Practical Strategies for Lighter Living

This section explores practical strategies for shedding the weight of excess in various aspects of life, enabling individuals to embrace a lighter existence. you are presented with actionable steps for decluttering physical spaces, simplifying daily routines, and minimizing commitments that no longer align with your values or priorities. Insights into embracing minimalism, mindful consumption, and intentional living practices are provided, empowering individuals to let go of what no longer serves them and create space for what truly matters.

The chapter also encourages you to declutter your mental and emotional spaces, fostering mindfulness, practicing self-care, and nurturing positive thought patterns. Strategies for managing stress, cultivating gratitude, and embracing self-compassion are discussed, enabling individuals to cultivate a lighter, more peaceful inner state.

Embracing Purpose: Crafting a Meaningful Life

The final segment delves into the pursuit of embracing purpose and crafting a meaningful life. It guides you in identifying your core values, passions, and aspirations, encouraging them to align your actions and choices accordingly. Insights into setting meaningful goals, fostering personal growth, and cultivating a sense of purpose in daily life are provided, enabling individuals to live with intentionality and direction.

The chapter emphasizes the significance of pursuing activities that bring joy, fulfillment, and a sense of meaning. It encourages you to explore new experiences, nurture your creativity, and contribute to causes or communities that resonate with your values. By embracing purpose, individuals can infuse every aspect of your lives with a sense of fulfillment and significance.

By embarking on the journey of embracing a lighter, more purposeful life, individuals not only shed the weight of excess but also cultivate a deeper sense of contentment, fulfillment, and alignment with their true selves.

In the pursuit of transformation towards a lighter, more purposeful life, this chapter serves as a comprehensive guide, offering practical strategies, insightful perspectives, and a deep understanding of the profound connection between intentional living and personal fulfillment. Through shedding the weight of excess, embracing purpose, and crafting a meaningful life, you are empowered to embark on a transformative journey, ultimately creating a life that reflects your values, passions, and aspirations.